Purple Turtle™

Roxy Learns to Swim

By Gail Skroback Hennessey

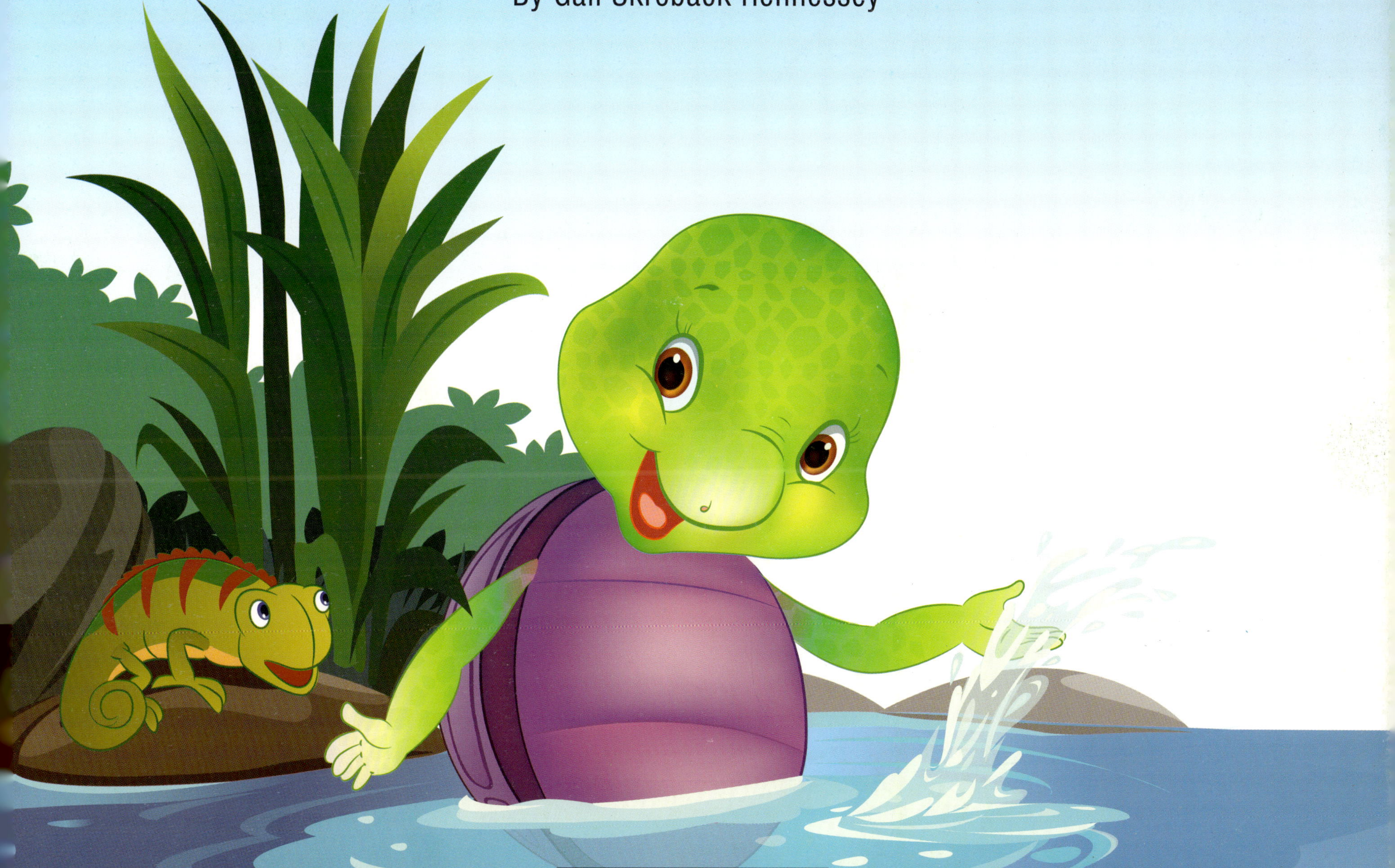

One beautiful day Purple and Roxy were sitting on a riverbank, with their feet dipped into the water.

"Let us go for a swim!" suggested Purple.

"I am not very fond of water as I am too scared of drowning," replied Roxy. "I will just watch you."

"Gee, Roxy, I didn't know that," said Purple. Roxy's head drooped in embarrassment.

"But hey! It is OK," said Purple.

"We all have our fears," said Purple. "I don't like being alone, I am glad I have friends like you."

"Go ahead, Purple! You should go and swim," said Roxy.

As Purple was standing in the water, he felt a tickle as a fish swam by his feet.

"Hello there! I am Fella," said the jolly fish poking her head out of the water.

“My name is Purple. It is nice to meet you,” replied Purple.

“It would be fun to play with you in the river,” swished Fella as she circled around Purple’s feet.

Purple watched Fella jump out of the water and dive back down several times.

Fella looked over to where Roxy was sitting– by the edge of the river.

"Hello! My name is Fella. Won't you come join us and play?"

"Thanks Fella, but I would prefer sitting here," answered Roxy.

Fella thought Roxy was not being very friendly. Then, Purple whispered to her that Roxy did not care for water as he was too scared of drowning.

“I wish I could get him overcome his fear,” Purple thought for a moment. “I think I have an idea! I need your help Fella.”

“Sure, I would love to help,” replied Fella.

“Roxy, what if you climb on top of my shell? Your feet will barely touch the water,” assured Purple.

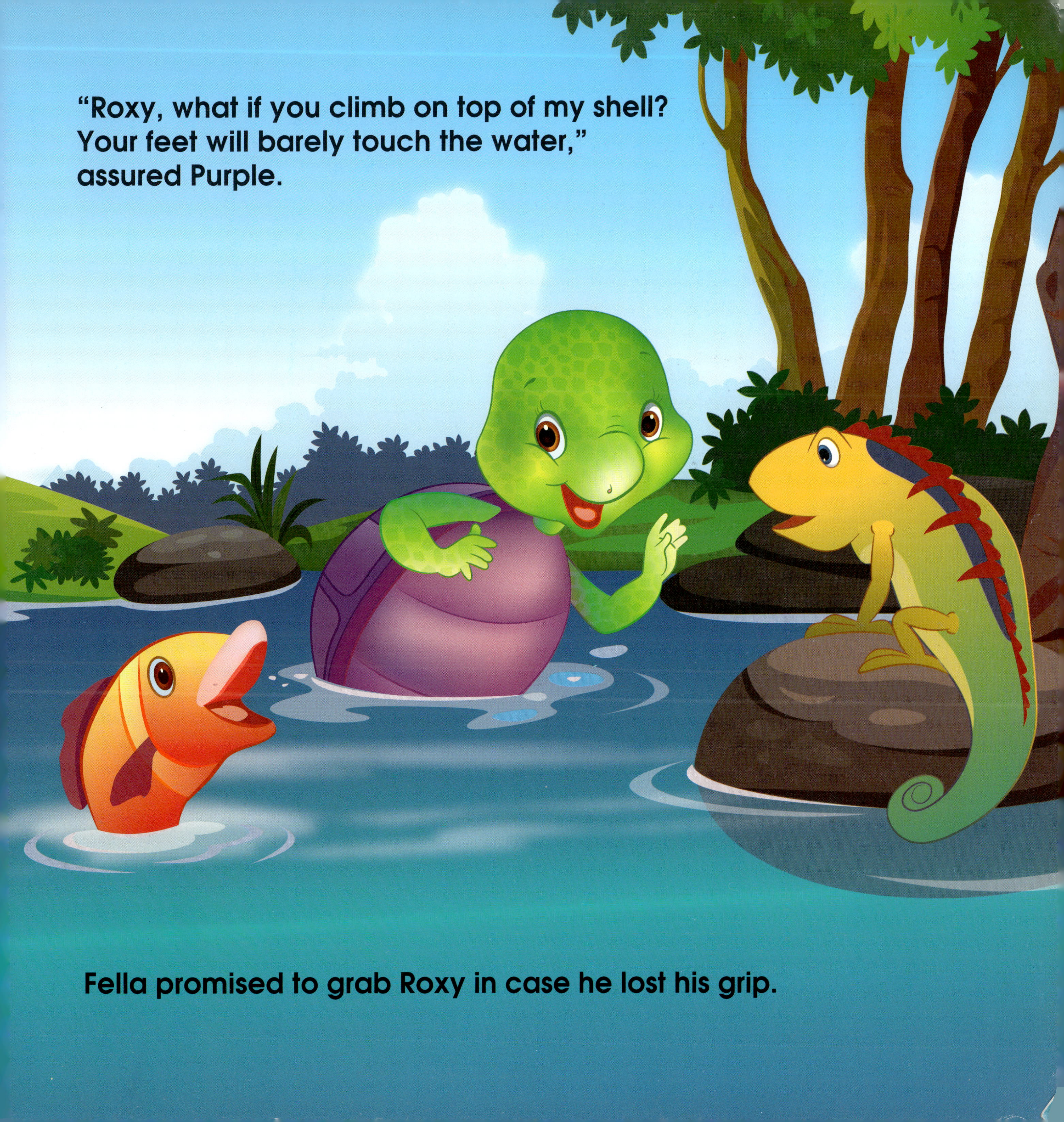

Fella promised to grab Roxy in case he lost his grip.

"Gee, I don't know," said Roxy. "I guess I can try."

Roxy inched his way down to the river's edge. He hesitated and then jumped onto Purple's back.

“Away we go,” shouted Purple, Fella swam alongside.

At first, Roxy was a bit frightened, slowly he began to smile.

“Wish I could swim but I am too scared of drowning,” he said.
“Purple, can you give me a swimming lesson?”

“Great idea Roxy! All you have to do is move your hands and legs just like I do,” said Purple.

“As Roxy learns to swim, I will be right underneath,” added Fella.

Roxy slowly got into the water and splashed as he tried to swim. "This is so much fun!" said Roxy. Fella helped him stay afloat. "I can swim! I can swim!" exclaimed Roxy.

"Roxy, you don't look like you are afraid of the water anymore," said Fella who was now Purple and Roxy's new friend.

"If we let our fears win, we miss out on a lot of fun," said Purple.